YOUR KNOWLEDGE HAS VALUE

Bibliographic information published by the German National Library:

The German National Library lists this publication in the National Bibliography; detailed bibliographic data are available on the Internet at http://dnb.dnb.de .

Imprint:

Copyright © 2019 GRIN Verlag
Print and binding: Books on Demand GmbH, Norderstedt Germany
ISBN: 9783668960176

Benjamin Heppner

Does the dual health insurance system produce a imbalanced access to health provision?

A reflection of outpatient care under ethical aspects

GRIN Verlag

GRIN - Your knowledge has value

Since its foundation in 1998, GRIN has specialized in publishing academic texts by students, college teachers and other academics as e-book and printed book. The website www.grin.com is an ideal platform for presenting term papers, final papers, scientific essays, dissertations and specialist books.

Visit us on the internet:

http://www.grin.com/

http://www.facebook.com/grincom

http://www.twitter.com/grin_com

Does the dual health insurance system produce a imbalanced access to health provision?

A reflection of outpatient care under ethical aspects.

Benjamin Heppner

Abstract

The dual health insurance system consists of statutory health insurance (SHI) and private full health insurance (PHI) in Germany is unique in Europe. About 72 million people in Germany are covered by one of the 110 statutory health insurances and around 9 million by the private sector. In 2016, a total of around 356.5 billion euros were spent for healthcare. Outpatient treatment in doctors' practices accounted for 14.9% of this total. Different research papers has shown, that the waiting time for a treatment is a indicator to measure imbalance access to health services. In two reports, different waiting times for SHI and PHI insured persons at a doctor's appointment could be determined. The length also depends on the distance to the end of the quarter, which is due to different rates paid to the doctors. This unequal treatment was considered from an ethical point of view from the point of view of Utilitarianism and Kantianism. Both legitimize this procedure, but it must be questioned whether a fundamental change would not be more beneficial. However, the different access to health care does not represent a lower quality of medical treatment. Recent studies have shown that SHI insurants even receive the better benefits and that there is only a difference in service.

Keywords: health-insurance-system, outpatient-care, utilitarianism, kantianism, ethics

Table of Contents

Does the dual health insurance system produce a imbalanced access to health provision?

A reflection of outpatient care under ethical aspects.

Introduction

The dual health insurance system consists of statutory health insurance (SHI) and private full health insurance (PHI) in Germany is unique in Europe. About 72 million people in Germany are covered by one of the 110 statutory health insurances and around 9 million by the private sector.

The headlines that keep coming up are placing PHI at the centre of debates about fair or equal treatment for the different patient groups, which has meanwhile led to the demand for a citizens' insurance as first defined by SPD. In a different characteristic also the "Grüne" and "LINKE" pursue a citizen insurance (Kröger, 2018). Health expenditures in Germany amount to 1 billion euros per day and average 4,330 euros for each inhabitant. This corresponds to 11.3% of the gross domestic product (GDP) (Statistische Bundesamt, 2018).

The outpatient sector was selected on the basis of medical progress in view of the ever-increasing number of treatments (Gibis & Tophoven, 2017, p. 191). These include SHI-accredited physicians, dentists, pharmacies and outpatient care institutions (Simon, 2017, p. 83). The shortage of resources of money and of doctors in the German healthcare system necessitates that decision-makers balance the efficiency and the costs of established medical services (Kopf-Schiller & Rottenkolber, 2014, p. 135). As a result of the economization of medicine in this field in recent years, the current progress in Germany in the area of inpatient and outpatient medicine would not be achieved (Jörg, 2015, p. 14). However, regardless of the success, the question also arises as to whether unequal payment by doctors based on the patient's insurance status also leads to unequal treatment of the patient (Jörg, 2015, p. 41).

Doctors once swore the Hippocratic Oath, which is now no longer a necessary condition for the final approbation. What effect does the dual health insurance have on medical care in the outpatient sector, which stakeholder groups are still affected in addition to patients, and what is the ethical outcome?

Answering these issues, the terms morality and ethics are defined below and two prominent ethical viewpoints, utilitarianism and Kant's categorical imperative, are introduced. In the following, an overview of the German health insurance system is given and the differences between PHI and SHI. This will serve as a base to explore the question of a different access to health provision as a result of the different insurance status. At the end, the results are summarized and reviewed under the described ethical principles.

Morals and Ethics

The expressions morality and ethics are sometimes used synonymously in daily life, which is incorrect. Therefore, both terms are clearly defined in the following. The expression morality is to be understood as the set of rules, notions, convictions and institutions that judge whether an action or institution is unjustified or justified and evil or good. It also judges whether a person has a virtuous or a good character or not. Morality can be defined as the sum of the aspects of rules, ideas, institutions and beliefs by which a person is judged (Steinvorth, 1999, p. 25). The designation and classification of good and evil is, however, strongly influenced by the observer's judgment. Nonetheless, it is still possible to make a statement that has a tendency towards both, because mostly good and evil are related to the effect on third parties. Therefore, an action is good when it benefits others and bad when it harms them (Conrad, 2016, pp. 9–10).

Moral norms therefore standardize behaviour and are based on generally recognized core values. The reflection of morality is ethics.

It should help to judge and weigh up in the sense of a "thus or that", to set up and evaluate alternatives for acting. This, however, is not in the sense of a "just thus", whereby certain acts are enforced with compulsion or by pressure and other are excluded (Jäggi, 2018, p. 16). This critical reflection of morality finally results in ethics and is the scientific theory of morality. It takes part on many levels. This is the organizational level, the level towards third parties, the interpersonal level and the individual level, known as Moral Intelligence. We can see that ethics is much more complex than morality, making it neither valid for the general public nor easily legitimizable by institutions or other individuals (Kartini, Reichert, Rüb, & Savanin, 2018, p. 4).

Ethics can be understood as a theory that describes and justifies the aspects of morality (Steinvorth, 1999, p. 26). The adherence to a value system with the core values of human dignity, justice, charity, well-being, equality, autonomy, honesty and transparency is to be understood as ethical behaviour (Jörg, 2015, p. 8). Ethics can affect a moral and even become a moral, but it has to be differentiated from a moral. Generally, it can be stated that every human being is necessarily following a moral, but does not always knows ethics. Ethics can be understood as the grammar of morality (Steinvorth, 1999, p. 26).

Business is increasingly under scrutiny with regard to ethical or unethical practices. Companies are regularly evaluated there on the basis of responsible behaviour or condemned for failing to behave correctly (Kartini et al., 2018, p. 3).

Following the Utilitarianism and Kantianism will be examined. Centered around a single major principle, both meld a variety of moral considerations into a surprisingly systematized

6

framework. Much is appealing in these theories, and they were the important models in ethical theory throughout much of the 20th century (Beauchamp, Bowie, & Arnold, 2009, p. 30).

Utility-based ethics by Bentham and Mill

All theories by which a measure of good or morally positive value can be given to actions and institutions, or how they produce happiness or desired circumstances, are utilitarian. Theories differ in the definition of happiness, the calculation of its magnitude, the comparison of alternative actions, and the definition of actions. But basically they agree that the moral quality of an action is measured by the magnitude of a positive circumstance created by it, for the one who enjoys it, is of no importance (Steinvorth, 1999, pp. 39–40). Evaluating the consequences of actions on others allows to balance them. The most extreme concept in the form of a quantitative balancing of consequences in utilitarianism was developed by Jeremy Bentham, the pioneer of this theory (Conrad, 2016, pp. 33–34). His idea was, that utilitarianism is bounded to the maximization of the good and the minimization of harm and evil. It states that society needs always to establish the greatest possible balance of positive value or minimum unbalance for all persons concerned. The key to maximization is efficiency, a congenial goal for business people because it is highly valued throughout the economic sector. Many companies and authorities have adopted specific tools such as cost-benefit analysis, risk assessment or target-oriented management, which are all strongly influenced by a utilitarian philosophy. A further essential feature of utilitarian theory is a theory of goodness.

Efficiency alone is simply as an instrumental good, i.e. it is strictly considered valuable as a means to something else. Even expansion and profit maximization are only instruments to the end of intrinsic goods.

7

Utilitarianism based solely on subjective preferences is therefore only satisfactory if a number of acceptable preferences can be formulated. Preferences that serve to block the preferences of others would then be disqualified by the ideal of utilitarianism (Beauchamp et al., 2009, pp. 19–21).

Bentham thought that all people have one ultimate goal: to be happy. For this reason, this view is typically labeled hedonic utilitarianism as Bentham understands the utility as happiness (Scharding, 2018, p. 52).

Mill, in contrast to Bentham, has a different vision of utilitarianism. He thought that the aim is not as simple as happiness maximization. In the sense that he thinks that something other, then purely (physical) happiness, is the most valuable thing, ethically spoken, we could call Mill a non-hedonic utilitarian. From Mill's point of view, decision-makers must ensure that their decisions protect certain very valuable ethical ideals. As a utilitarian, Mill believes these ideals create utility. He uses the concepts of higher and lower pleasures, to distinguish these more and less valuable kinds of utility. Lower pleasures are always trumped by higher once. In Mill's utilitarian calculus, they must always count for more, quantitatively (Scharding, 2018, p. 57).

Utilitarian moral philosophers can be conventionally split into two groups - Act Utilitarians and Rule Utilitarians. An act utilitarian argues that in all situations the activity leading to the greatest benefit for most people should be performed. However, the rule utilitarian reserves a more valuable place for rules that he does not consider dispensable in order to maximize utility in a particular circumstance. His actions are thus justified by the appeal to abstract rules such as "do not kill", "do not bribe" and "do not break promise". Utilitarian rules are theoretically firm and protect all classes of individuals, just as human rights are rigidly protective of all individuals, independent of social convenience and momentary necessity (Beauchamp et al., 2009, pp. 21–22).

An act utilitarian argues that in all situations the activity leading to the greatest benefit for most people should be performed. However, the rule utilitarian reserves a more valuable place for rules that he does not consider dispensable in order to maximize utility in a particular circumstance. His actions are thus justified by the appeal to abstract rules such as "do not kill", "do not bribe" and "do not break promise". Utilitarian rules are theoretically firm and protect all classes of individuals, just as human rights are rigidly protective of all individuals, independent of social convenience and momentary necessity (Beauchamp et al., 2009, pp. 21–22).

Whether preference units or other utilitarian values such as happiness can be measured and compared to determine the best action among alternatives is a major problem for utilitarianism. Utilitarianism has also been criticized on the basis that it does ignore non-utilitarian factors that are required for moral decisions. In the long run, utilitarian argue that promoting utility does not produce overall unequal outcomes (Beauchamp et al., 2009, pp. 22–23).

In the contemporary debate on utilitarianism sufficient arguments are produced which make it impossible to recognize the aspiration of classical utilitarianism. Too many and too deep moral institutions disagree with place increasing the welfare of a society or the entire human race over all other possible aspects (Steinvorth, 1999, p. 40).

9

Kant's duty-based ethics

Nowadays, the universal principles of validity of ethics established by Kant are still valid and are experiencing a new flourishing in "New Kantianism". According to Kant, the human mind remains the original legislator of nature when nature is understood to mean the principles of phenomena in time and space (Wühle, 2015, p. 6).

While Bentham and Mill base their views on utility, Kant believes that the most important ethical value is duty. For Kant, the measure of ethical action is not maximizing happiness, it is acting in accordance with one's own duties. Like utilitarianism, Kant's standard has an intuitive appeal: it is easy to understand why Kant believes that it is right to fulfill one's duties. Finally, a duty is something we have to do - so it seems obvious that we should fulfill our duties (Scharding, 2018, p. 61). Kant argued that individuals should be treated as goals and never only as means to the end of others. In other words, disregarding individuals means treating them as a means to their own ends, as if they were not independent actors. Showing a lack of respect for a person means either rejecting the person's considered judgments, ignoring the person's concerns and needs, or denying the person the ability to respond to those judgments. Kant did not categorically outlaw the use of individuals as a means to benefit other people. He argued only that individuals should not treat another exclusively as a means to their end. Kant only seems to demand that each individual will accept these principles. If a person willingly accepts a certain form of action and it is not immoral in itself, that person is a free being and has the right to choose it. Kant's theory finds that motives for action to be of most importance by expecting people to make the right decisions for the right reasons (Beauchamp et al., 2009, pp. 24–25). Kant asserted that moral action must be motivated by a maxim (rule) of moral self-commitment. Kant stressed that all individuals must act in the name of that commitment - not simply in accordance with that commitment. Kant developed this concept into a fundamental moral law: 'I ought never to act except in such a way that I also want my maxim to become a universal law'. Kant called this axiom the categorical imperative. It is categorical because it permits all exceptions and is absolutely binding. It is imperative because it provides instructions about how one must conduct oneself (Beauchamp et al., 2009, pp. 26–27).

For example, customers should not only be seen as a means of making a profit by selling the products to them, rather they should also take into consideration the impact of the product to each of them, e.g. not selling rotten meat to them. Kant also refers this to the actor himself. He should not regard himself as a means, but also as an end, in other words he should not harm himself (Conrad, 2016, p. 24).

But there is also criticism of Kant's categorical imperative. For example, Altman has criticized ethical theories which in particular can only evaluate the actions of individual actors. He concentrates on Kant's ethics in particular. First, Altman argues that enterprises are not morally responsible from a Kantian point of view. Enterprises lack the attributes that moral persons require, for Kant. These characteristics include inclination and rationality. Second, he argues that Kant is also struggling to assign moral responsibility that is so prevalent throughout the enterprise that it is impossible to bind it to anyone in particular (Scharding, 2018, p. 88). The Kantian ethic is also often criticized as narrow and not sufficient to handle various problems in moral life. Some people also argue that Kant has emphasized universal duties (duties that are common to all individuals) at the expense of special duties (duties that apply only to those in specific relationships or roles, such as managing directors). However, special duties and relations may not conflict with Kantianism as they may not violate universal ethical norms. A related aspect of Kant's ethical theory, examined by philosophers, is his view that moral motivation involves impartial principles. Impartial motivation can be differentiated from the motivation a person might have to treat a second person in a particular way because the first person has a special interest in the second person's well-being (e.g. the spouse or valued client). In conclusion, there is almost no moral philosopher who today finds Kant's system completely satisfactory. Defenders tend to say that Kant provides the main elements of a sound moral position (Beauchamp et al., 2009, pp. 27–29).

The German health insurance system

The German health insurance system began on June 15th, 1883, by Otto von Bismarck, the "Chancellor of the Reich" who enacted the law on workers' health insurance. From that point forward, industrial workers and employees in craft and trade enterprises were obliged to be covered by health insurance. From this time onwards, SHI was developed into a comprehensive social security system and adjusted to the new challenges faced by the time. It is the central element of the German health system and the oldest sector of social insurance (Bundesministerium für Gesundheit, 2018).

The German concept of two health care systems, consisting of SHI and PHI sectors, is more than 130 years old. This dual form of insurance currently covers 48 (Lullies, 2018) private and 110 statutory health insurance companies. 8.75 million people are covered by PHI, the majority with 72.23 million are covered by SHI (Statista GmbH, 2018).

In 2016, a total of around 356.5 billion euros were spent for healthcare. Outpatient treatment in doctors' practices accounted for 14.9% of this total. In addition, the state supported the SHI companies with 58.1% and the PHI companies with 8.7% of the incurred expenses (Statistische Bundesamt, 2018).

Medical care and the guarantee of it are accorded an extraordinarily high priority by the jurisdiction of the Federal Constitutional Court (Huster, 2010, p. 238). The right to access healthcare is established internationally and nationally. It refers on the one hand to individual health care and on the other hand to the safeguarding of external framework conditions and opportunities for collective participation (Hirschberg & Strech, 2010, p. 18).

Statutory health insurance vs. private health insurance

The access to the dual insurance system with SHI and PHI is regulated according to the salary level or civil servant status, which is disavowing for the individual person and justifies a two-class medicine (Jörg, 2015, p. 52). Employees who exceed the annual threshold of 60.750 euros for health insurance in 2019 may, after a waiting period of one year, switch from SHI to PHI or continue to voluntarily insure in SHI (DAK-Gesundheit, 2018).

In PHI, the policyholder can set his own priorities and thus minimize the fee. At the same time, the insurance company can also charge risk surcharges or exclude services, which is not always beneficial for the policyholder (Jörg, 2015, p. 52). With the contract conclusion a two-sided connection with the PHI develops. A contract for the requested services is concluded directly with the physician or a hospital, the medical service provider. The health insurance company repays the costs to the private patient against proof, in contractual extent. This is called the cost reimbursement principle (Karakas, 2014, p. 10). The access restrictions mentioned at the beginning may lead to considerable injustices, which can even go so far that persons with compulsory SHI insurance pay a higher monthly fee than comparable persons with a significantly higher salary in the private health insurance system.

Conversely, the rates in private health insurance increase disproportionately in old age as opposed to the SHI system, which is due to risk selection, inadequate risk structure compensation and the unlimited entitlement mentality of patients as well as the prescription frenzy of expensive medical services by doctors (Jörg, 2015, p. 53).

In the SHI system, on the other hand, health services are provided within the framework of the so-called principle of benefits in kind. Here, the physicians conclude contracts with the SHI which commit them to pay the remuneration agreed upon (Simon, 2017, p. 65).

In this context, services which are not necessary or uneconomical are to be refused to the insured persons, not to be effected by the service providers and not to be authorised by the health insurance funds (Kopf-Schiller & Rottenkolber, 2014, p. 136). Accordingly, the principle of covering needs applies, whereby insured persons are legally entitled to all medically necessary services. These must be sufficient and appropriate, correspond to the general state of medical expertise and take medical progress into account. They are not allowed to exceed what is necessary and must be provided economically (Simon, 2017, pp. 112–113). It should be noted that the PHI pay more services than the SHI (Karakas, 2014, p. 12).

Different access for outpatient care

It is regularly said that SHI insured persons have a less favourable access to health services than persons with private health insurance. But how does this look? On the one hand, people with private health insurance receive a more comprehensive diagnosis, especially in the outpatient sector with the same disease status. This is the result of the fact that PHI often pays more than double for the same medical services as SHI. This difference brings every doctor into a conflict of interest.

Regardless of the fulfillment of the patient's well-being as the primary goal, doctors develop secondary goals such as higher service, faster appointments and more complex diagnostics (Jörg, 2015, p. 14). At the end of a therapy, the doctor informs the SHI patient, but usually does not provide extensive information. In addition, the duration of the consultation is often shorter than with a PHI patient.

This can be illustrated using the example of a resting ECG and findings. The doctor receives a quarterly flat-rate payment of approximately 30 euros from the SHI. In the case of a PHI insured person, 2.3 to 3.5 rates can be charged for the same benefit in accordance with the scale of fees for physicians (GOÄ), which corresponds to approximately 80 euros. Another example of overdiagnostics is the per-capita laboratory costs in 2008, which amounted to 26 euros for those with statutory insurance and 129 euros for people with private insurance (Jörg, 2015, p. 27).

The Standard Valuation Scale (EBM) is used for the quarterly accounting of SHI insured persons. The services performed are converted into points, which then determine the invoice amount. This also depends on the budget volume and the regional affiliation of the Association of Statutory Health Insurance Physicians (Jörg, 2015, p. 64). That means that Physicians are subjected to budget limits on an individual level, called standard benefit volume (RLV).

It defines the maximum quantity of services that a physician can charge without any discount. At a much lower rate services performed if the budget limits are reimbursed (Heinrich, Wübker, & Wuckel, p. 8). In addition to services within the RLV, there are certain services which are always reimbursed at full prices. Some examples are prevention services, outpatient surgery and vaccinations (Himmel & Schneider, 2017, p. 4).

Due to the different billing modalities according to GOÄ and EBM, different fees are concealed despite the same medical services (Jörg, 2015, p. 100). This can lead to a so-called supply induced demand, as it depends largely on the physician. The full health insurance systems and medical developments in particular favour this process. In this case, the patient's willingness to pay does not play a role, as it does not serve to limit consumption. Modern diagnostic techniques allow doctors to prescribe wide-ranging therapies in which the patient does not suffer any deterioration in benefit despite increased consumption. This does not lead to complete consumer sovereignty, because the patient usually only determines the first contact, but the physician defines the further scope of the medical services (Udo & Schneider, p. 45). The goal of medical action is often to maximize profits and achieve a certain target income (Udo & Schneider, pp. 45–46). Here the argument of fairness, which is the ideal of approval, is violated and carried out under fair background conditions. It is one of the primary arguments for using markets to allocate goods. Respect for the freedom of choice. It gives individuals the opportunity to decide for their own (Himmel & Schneider, 2017, p. 5).

It was to find out how far the waiting period for an appointment at the end of the quarter would change if the RLVs had already been allocated by the doctors. Already 28-15 days before the end of the quarter, appointments for which billable services related to the RLV were incurred were only allocated for the following quarter. This increased the waiting period by a further 8.71 to 14.15 percent. Dates for directly billable services that are not covered by the RLV were noticeably brought forward (Himmel & Schneider, 2017, pp. 14–15).

Another survey for the years 2014 to 2016 showed that the average waiting time for SHI patients increased from 27.5 days in 2014 to up to 30.7 days at the peak.

PHI patients, on the other hand, even experienced a reduction in the average waiting time from 13.5 days in 2014 to 7.8 days in 2016 (Heinrich et al., p. 3). 33.5 percent of SHI survey respondents stated that a waiting period of at least two weeks was subjectively perceived as too long. At 14.7 percent, the dissatisfaction among PHI policyholders is significantly lower, but still there, despite a significantly shorter waiting time (Zok, 2007, p. 1).

PHI insurants have a higher income and therefore the opportunity costs of the waiting period are higher than SHI insurants. This means that private patients change doctors much more quickly, which means that doctors prefer this customer group accordingly (Heinrich et al., p. 8). In addition, there is the incentive for the doctors' practices that the services provided to PHI patients are usually due immediately and invoiced, which is also important for the liquidity of the practice. In contrast, SHI pays only once a quarter. This also leads to the fact that the average share of 10 percent of privately insured persons in the practices generates a quarter of the revenue, which is also due to the higher possibilities for accounting (Jörg, 2015, p. 30).

Utilitarianism states the greatest benefit for the greatest number. Applied to this example, the approach is ethically justified. The medical practices earn a quarter of their turnover with PHI patients, which are paid out regularly. Due to the higher chargeable services, new, modern medical equipment can also be made available, which also benefits the SHI patients. This also promotes the corresponding economy and industry from a macroeconomic point of view. Furthermore, the practice also secures the PHI patient base through preferential treatment, which does not like to wait long and is otherwise willing to change practices rapidly. All participants "win". SHI patients "also pay" for a correspondingly modern equipment with a longer waiting time, which they nevertheless get paid by SHI.

In this context, however, the supply-induced demand for services on the part of physicians could be seen as unethical, as excessive diagnostics unnecessarily burden the health insurance system, which is reflected in rising health insurance contributions in the PHI sector. It is unclear to what extent both will be offset against each other, so that the greatest benefit will continue to apply to the largest number.

The oath of the Hippocrates also places the doctor-patient relationship on a personal basis of trust. The advice and treatment provided by the doctor should generally be independent of financial considerations or administrative instructions, but in most cases this is no longer the position (Jörg, 2015, p. 58).

Kant wrote: 'Act only according to that maxim by which you can at the same time want it to become a general law' (Conrad, 2016, p. 25). This is also known as the categorical imperative, which was previously presented in the paper. If behaviour is applied that is also generally applied in society, then the preferential treatment of PHI patients in doctor's practices is ethically justifiable in the Kantian view. It is well known in society that PHI insurants earn more money, have less time and receive priority according to their status in health insurance. This is also reflected in the practices that represent it in society and back again. But it should rather be thought about whether the category of this thinking should not be altered. There are already first medical practices that do not differentiate between SHI and PHI anymore, except in the accounting to be done. Perhaps the principle "all people are equal" (also found in the German Basic Law) should be applied and then treated equally. For this, however, the economic interests of the individual players are still too prominent.

Politics and research have already addressed this issue and made a number of requirements. Starting with the unified citizens' insurance system mentioned above (Jörg, 2015,

p. 66), through the harmonisation of the payment of benefits (Jörg, 2015, p. 40) to stronger enforcement and pursuit of medical ethics (Jäger, 2014, p. 67).

Conclusion

The research has shown that there is a difference in access to medical services for outpatient care if the waiting time for an appointment is used as a measure. The duality of two health insurance systems and the different accounting methods sometimes lead to the idea of a return on investment becoming predominant and to primary professional ethical goals such as patient well-being and the well-being of employees taking equal priority over economic goals. Privately insured persons are "over-benefited" financially in such a way that the SHI patients are cross-funded (Jörg, 2015, p. 9).

Every year, over 33 billion euros flow through PHI insurants into the healthcare system, ensuring high medical standards for both PHI and SHI insurants (Verband der Privaten Krankenversicherung e. V.).

If economics action continues to develop to the disadvantage of doctors and patients over the next few years, medical autonomy must be restored by separating any medical activity from financial incentives (Jörg, 2015, pp. 19–20).

Doctors who settle down and thus join the Association of Statutory Health Insurance Physicians also decide to treat those insured by statutory health insurance. The contributions of the 72 million SHI insurants alone make it possible for PHI patients to receive comprehensive care (beb/dpa, 2018).

Despite all the negative press and headlines about the dual insurance system, it performs much better in terms of quality of care. The difference has practically no effect on the quality of care or life expectancy (Jörg, 2015, p. 62). Rather, we should speak of a different level of service rather than focusing on the quality of medical care. There are also studies that clearly disprove that SHI is only second class. On the contrary, many of the PHI's plans cannot guarantee even basic services. It also showed that even in expensive premium plans, fewer services are consistently offered than in the SHI (Kröger, 2018).

References

Beauchamp, T. L., Bowie, N. E., & Arnold, D. G. (2009). *Ethical theory and business* (8th ed.). London: Pearson Education LTD.

Beb/dpa. (2018). Bevorzugung von Privatpatienten - Krankenkassen fordern Strafen für Ärzte.

Bundesministerium für Gesundheit. (2018). Geschichte der gesetzlichen Krankenversicherung. Retrieved from https://www.bundesgesundheitsministerium.de/themen/krankenversicherung/grundprinzipien/geschichte.html

Conrad, C. A. (2016). *Wirtschaftsethik: Eine Voraussetzung für Produktivität. Lehrbuch.* Wiesbaden: Springer Gabler.

DAK-Gesundheit. (2018). Versicherungspflichtig Beschäftigte. Retrieved from https://www.dak.de/dak/beitraege/versicherungspflichtig-beschaeftigte-1100282.html

Gibis, B., & Tophoven, C. (2017). Reformbedarf in der ambulanten Versorgung: Dauerthema der Gesundheitspolitik. In A. Brandhorst, H. Hildebrandt, & E.-W. Luthe (Eds.), *Gesundheit. Politik - Gesellschaft - Wirtschaft. Kooperation und Integration – das unvollendete Projekt des Gesundheitssystems* (pp. 191–213). Wiesbaden: Springer Fachmedien Wiesbaden.

Heinrich, N., Wübker, A., & Wuckel, C. Waiting times for outpatient treatment in Germany: New experimental evidence from primary data, Bochum, Germany.

Himmel, K., & Schneider, U. (2017). *Ambulatory care at the end of a billing period* (HCHE Research Paper No. 2017/14). Retrieved from University of Hamburg website: http://hdl.handle.net/10419/157532

21

Hirschberg, I., & Strech, D. (2010). Public Health: Eine Einführung zur Theorie und Praxis der Disziplin. In D. Strech (Ed.), *Ethik im Gesundheitswesen: Bd. 1. Public-Health-Ethik* (pp. 15–42). Berlin, Münster: Lit.

Huster, S. (2010). Möglichkeiten und Grenzen rechtlicher Regulierung zur Durchsetzung von Public Health-Maßnahmen. In D. Strech (Ed.), *Ethik im Gesundheitswesen: Bd. 1. Public-Health-Ethik* (pp. 237–254). Berlin, Münster: Lit.

Jäger, C. (2014). Rechtliche und ethische Aspekte der Priorisierung in der Medizin. In A. Frewer (Ed.), *Jahrbuch Ethik in der Klinik: Vol. 7. Gute oder vergütete Behandlung? Ethische Fragen der Gesundheitsökonomie* (pp. 57–76). Würzburg: Königshausen & Neumann.

Jäggi, C. J. (2018). *Wirtschaftsordnung und Ethik: Problemfelder - Modelle - Lösungsansätze.* Wiesbaden: Springer Fachmedien Wiesbaden.

Jörg, J. (2015). *Berufsethos kontra Ökonomie: Haben wir in der Medizin zu viel Ökonomie und zu wenig Ethik?* Berlin: Springer-Verlag.

Karakas, L. (2014). *Gesetzliche vs. Private Krankenversicherung: Pro und Contra unter Berücksichtigung des deutschen Sozialstaatsmodells.* Hamburg: Bachelor + Master Publishing.

Kartini, V., Reichert, M., Rüb, M., & Savanin, T. (2018). *Unternehmensethische Ansätze für Business-Entscheidungen: Praxiswissen für die Führungsaufgabe. essentials.* Wiesbaden: Springer Gabler.

Kopf-Schiller, C., & Rottenkolber, D. (2014). Gute oder vergütete Behandlung? Der Medizinische Dienst der Krankenversicherung im Spannungsfeld von Ethik und Sozialgesetzgebung. In A. Frewer (Ed.), *Jahrbuch Ethik in der Klinik: Vol. 7. Gute oder vergütete Behandlung? Ethische Fragen der Gesundheitsökonomie* (pp. 135–156). Würzburg: Königshausen & Neumann.

Kröger, M. (2018). Versicherungen im Vergleich: Wo gesetzliche Krankenkassen besser sind als private - und wo nicht. Retrieved from http://www.spiegel.de/wirtschaft/soziales/krankenkassen-wo-gesetzliche-besser-sind-als-private-und-wo-nicht-a-1245687.html

Lullies, D. (2018). Private Krankenversicherung Anzahl der Unternehmen. Retrieved from http://www.gbe-bund.de/oowa921-install/servlet/oowa/aw92/dboowasys921.xwdevkit/xwd_init?gbe.isgbetol/xs_start_neu/&p_aid=i&p_aid=80439715&nummer=242&p_sprache=D&p_indsp=-&p_aid=37926620

Scharding, T. (2018). *This is business ethics: An introduction. This is philosophy.* Hoboken, NJ: Wiley Blackwell.

Simon, M. (2017). *Das Gesundheitssystem in Deutschland: Eine Einführung in Struktur und Funktionsweise* (6., vollständig aktualisierte und überarbeitete Auflage). Bern: Hogrefe.

Statista GmbH. (2018). Themenseite: Krankenversicherung. Retrieved from https://de.statista.com/themen/649/krankenversicherung/

Statistische Bundesamt. (2018). Staat & Gesellschaft - Gesundheitsausgaben. Retrieved from https://www.destatis.de/DE/ZahlenFakten/GesellschaftStaat/Gesundheit/Gesundheitsausgaben/Gesundheitsausgaben.html

Steinvorth, U. (1999). Angewandte Ethik und Zivilgesellschaft. In G. Brudermüller (Ed.), *Schriften des Instituts für Angewandte Ethik e.V: Bd. 1. Angewandte Ethik und Medizin* (pp. 25–48). Würzburg: Königshausen & Neumann.

Udo, S., & Schneider, U. Theorie und Empirie der Arzt-Patient-Beziehung: Zur Anwendung der Principial-Agent-Theorie auf die Gesundheitsnachfrage // Theorie und Empirie der Arzt-Patient-Beziehung (Dissertation). Universität Greifswald.

Verband der Privaten Krankenversicherung e. V. PKV im Gesundheitssystem. Retrieved from https://www.pkv.de/themen/krankenversicherung/pkv-im-gesundheitssystem/

Wühle, M. (2015). *Die Moral der Märkte*. Dissertation.

Zok, K. (2007). *Warten auf den Arzttermin: Ergebnisse einer Repräsentativumfrage unter GKV- und PKV-Versicherten* (WIdOmonitor). Bonn. Retrieved from Wissenschaftliches Institut der AOK (WidO) website: http://www.wido.de

YOUR KNOWLEDGE HAS VALUE

- We will publish your bachelor's and master's thesis, essays and papers

- Your own eBook and book - sold worldwide in all relevant shops

- Earn money with each sale

Upload your text at www.GRIN.com and publish for free